THE

BOW IN THE CLOUD,

OR,

WORDS OF COMFORT FOR HOURS OF SORROW.

BY THE AUTHOR OF

"THE MORNING AND NIGHT WATCHES,"
"PALMS OF ELIM," &c. &c.

One Hundred and Sixtieth Thousand

LONDON:
JAMES NISBET & CO., 21 BERNERS STREET.
MDCCCLXXX.

Ballantyne Press
BALLANTYNE, HANSON AND CO.
EDINBURGH AND LONDON

Printing Statement:

Due to the very old age and scarcity of this book,
many of the pages may be hard to read due to the
blurring of the original text, possible missing pages,
missing text, dark backgrounds and other issues
beyond our control.

Because this is such an important and rare work, we
believe it is best to reproduce this book regardless of
its original condition.

Thank you for your understanding.

"Blessed be God, even the Father of our Lord Jesus Christ, the Father of mercies, and the God of all comfort; who comforteth us in all our tribulation, that we may be able to comfort them which are in any trouble, by the comfort wherewith we ourselves are comforted of God." —2 Cor. 1. 3, 4.

"I do set this Bow in the Cloud"—

" The Lord reigneth."—Ps. xciii. 1.

Sovereignty. No Bow of Promise in "the dark and cloudy day" shines more radiantly than this.

God—my God—the God who gave *Jesus*,—orders all events, and overrules all for my good!

" *When I*," says He, " *bring a cloud over the earth.*" He has no wish to conceal the hand which shadows, for a time, earth's brightest prospects. It is He alike who "brings" the cloud, who brings us *into* it, and in mercy leads us *through* it. His kingdom ruleth over all. " *The lot is cast into the lap, but the whole disposing thereof is of the Lord.*" We are tenants at will; but, blessed thought, at *God's* will. He puts the burden on, and keeps it on, and at His own time will remove it.

Beware of brooding over second

causes. It is the worst form of athe-
ism. When our most fondly-cherished
gourds are smitten—when our fairest
flowers lie withered in our bosom—this
is the silencer of all reflections, "The
LORD prepared the worm." When the
Temple of the Soul is smitten with
lightning—its pillars rent—"*The* LORD
is in His holy Temple." Accident,
Chance, Fate, Destiny, have no place
in the Christian's creed. His is no unpiloted vessel, left to the mercy of the
storm,—no weed left to the sport of the
fitful waves. "*The voice of the* LORD
is upon the waters." "Fear not: IT IS
I , be not afraid." There is but one explanation of all that befals us: "*I will
be dumb, I will open not my mouth,
because* THOU *didst it.*"

DEATH to the human spectator, seems
the most capricious and wayward of
events. But not so. The keys of Hades
are in the hands of this same reigning
God. Look at the Parable of the Fig-

tree. Its prolonged existence, or its doom as a cumberer, forms matter of conversation in Heaven;—the axe cannot be laid at its root until God gives the warrant. How much more will this be the case regarding every "Tree of Righteousness, the planting of the Lord?" It will be watched over by Him, "lest any one should hurt it." Every trembling fibre He will care for; and if made early to succumb to the inevitable stroke, "*who knoweth not in all these, that the hand of the Lord hath wrought this?*" (Job xii. 9.)

Be it mine to merge my own will in His; not to cavil at His ways, or seek to have one jot or tittle of that will altered; but to lie passive in His hands;—to take the bitter as well as the sweet,—knowing that the cup is mingled by ONE, who loves me too well to add one ingredient that might have been spared. "We should say," says Philip Henry, "what pleases God, pleases me. As in active obedience, we do duty because it is His will to command; so, in passive endurance, we bear, because it is His will to inflict." "Nothing," says Jeremy Taylor, "does so establish the mind amidst the rollings and turbulence of present things, as both a look above them, and a look beyond them;—above them, to the steady and good hand by which they are ruled; and beyond them, to the sweet and beautiful end to which, *by* that hand, they will be brought."

Who can wonder, that the sweet Psalmist of Israel, as he sees it spanning the lowering heavens, should seek to fix the arrested gaze of a whole world on the softened tints of this Bow of Comfort—"THE LORD REIGNETH, LET THE EARTH REJOICE."

"AND IT SHALL COME TO PASS,
WHEN I BRING A CLOUD OVER THE EARTH, THAT
THE BOW SHALL BE SEEN IN THE CLOUD "

2D DAY.

"I do set this Bow in the Cloud"—

"The Lord hath pleasure in the prosperity of his servant."—Ps. xxxv. 27.

A Loving Purpose. WHAT is "Prosperity?" Is it the threads of life woven into a bright tissue? a full cup—ample riches—worldly applause—an unbroken circle? Nay, these are often a snare—received without gratitude—dimming the soul to its nobler destinies. Often, spiritually, it rather means, God taking us by the hand into the lowly Valleys of Humiliation; leading us, as He did his servant Job of old, out of his sheep, oxen, camels, health, wealth, children,—in order that we may be brought to lie before Him in the dust, and say, "*Blessed be His name!*"

Yes, the very reverse of what is known in the world as Prosperity (generally) forms the background on which the Bow of Promise is seen. God smiles on us through these rain-drops and

tear-drops of *Sorrow.* *He* loves us
too well — He has too great an in-
terest in our spiritual welfare, to permit
us to live on in what is *misnamed*
"Prosperity." When He sees duties
languidly performed, or coldly neglected,
—the heart deadened, and love to Himself congealed by the absorbing power
of a present world, He puts a thorn
in our nest to drive us to the wing,
and prevent our being grovellers for
ever!

I may not be able now, to understand
the mystery of these dealings. I may
be asking through tears, "Why this
unkind arrest on my earthly happiness?
Why so premature a lopping of my
boughs of promise? Such a speedy
withering of my most cherished gourd?"
The answer is plain. It is thy *Soul
Prosperity* He has in view. Believe it,
thy truest EBENEZERS will yet be raised
close by thy ZAREPHATHS ("the place
of furnaces"). His afflictions are no

arbitrary appointments. There is a righteous *necessity* in all He does. As He lays His chastening hand upon thee, and leads thee by ways thou knowest not, and which thou thyself never wouldst have chosen; He whispers the gentle accents in thine ear, "*Beloved, I wish above all things that thou mayst prosper and be in health.*"

Rest in the quiet consciousness that all is well. Murmur at nothing which brings thee nearer His own loving Presence. Be thankful for thy very cares, because thou canst confidingly cast them all upon Him. He has thy temporal and eternal "prosperity" too much at heart, to appoint one superfluous pang, one redundant stroke. Commit, therefore, all that concerns thee to His keeping, and leave it there.

"AND IT SHALL COME TO PASS,
WHEN I BRING A CLOUD OVER THE EARTH, THAT
THE BOW SHALL BE SEEN IN THE CLOUD."

"I do set this Bow in the Cloud"—

"A man shall be as an hiding-place from the wind, and a covert from the tempest ; as rivers of water in a dry place; as the shadow of a great rock in a weary land."—ISA. xxxii. 2.

The Safe Retreat. "A MAN." This first word forms the Key to this precious verse, It is "*The* MAN Christ Jesus."

And when and where is He thus revealed to His people as their "hiding-place?" It is, as with Elijah of old, in the whirlwind and the storm. Amid the world's bright sunshine, in the calm of tranquil skies—uninterrupted prosperity—they seek Him not. But when the clouds begin to gather, and the sun is swept from their firmament; when they have learned the insecurity of all earthly refuges, *then* the prayer ascends, "*My heart is overwhelmed, lead me to the* ROCK *that is higher than I.*" The Earthquake—the Tempest—the Fire—and *then* "the still small voice!"

Sorrowing believer, you have indeed a sure Covert—a strong Tower which cannot be shaken. The World has its coverts too. But they cannot stand the day of trial. The wind passeth over them, and they are gone. But the louder the hurricane, the more will it endear to you the abiding Shelter; the deeper in the clefts of this ROCK, the safer you are.

A MAN. Delight often to dwell on the Humanity of JESUS. You have a Brother on the Throne;—a " living Kinsman;"—One who "knoweth your frame;" and who, by the exquisite sympathies of His exalted Human nature, can gauge, as none other can, the depths of your sorrow.

An earthly friend comes to you in trial; he has never known bereavement, and therefore cannot enter into your woe. Another comes; he has been again and again in the Furnace; his heart has been touched tenderly as your own; he can feelingly sympathise with you. It is so with JESUS. As *Man*, He has passed through every experience of suffering. He has Himself known the storm from which He offers you shelter. He is the ROCK, yet "a MAN." "Mighty to save;" yet mighty to compassionate. "IMMANUEL, God with us!" He is like the Bow in the material Heavens, which, while its summit is in the clouds, either base of its arc rests on earth; or like the oak, which, while it can wrestle with the tempest, yet invites the feeblest bird to fold its wing on its branches.

Mourner, Go, sit under thy "Beloved's shadow with great delight." Test His ability and willingness to sustain and comfort thee, in the hour when the best of human solaces reveal their inadequacy. When the creature rill has failed, try the Infinite Fountain-head. Hide in His wounded side. The hand which was pierced for thee is ordering thy trials, He who roused the storm is the hiding-place from it. And as thou dost journey on—gloomy clouds mustering around thee—let *this* bright Bow of comfort ever arrest thy drooping eye— "*In all things it behoved Him to be made like unto His brethren. . . . For in that He Himself hath suffered, being tempted, He is able to succour them that are tempted.*"

"AND IT SHALL COME TO PASS, WHEN I BRING A CLOUD OVER THE EARTH, THAT THE BOW SHALL BE SEEN IN THE CLOUD."

"I do set this Bow in the Cloud"—

"Whom the Lord loveth he chasteneth."—HEB. xii. C.

The Reason for Chastisement. WHAT! God *loveth* me when He is discharging His quiver upon me,—emptying me from vessel to vessel,—causing the sun of my earthly joys to set in clouds? Yes, O afflicted, tossed with tempest—He *chastens* thee BECAUSE He *loves* thee. This trial comes from His own tender, loving hand,—His own tender unchanging heart!

Art thou laid on a *sick-bed*—are sorrowful months and wearisome nights appointed unto thee? Let this be the pillow on which thine aching head reclines—*It is because He loves me!*

Is it *bereavement* that has swept thy heart and desolated thy dwelling? He appointed that chamber of death—He opened that tomb—*because He loves thee!* As it is the suffering child of the family which claims a mother's deepest affections and most tender solicitude,—so hast thou at this moment embarked on thy side, the tenderest love and solicitude of a chastening Heavenly Father. He loved thee *into* this sorrow, and He will love thee *through* it. There is nothing arbitrary in His dealings. LOVE is the reason of all He does. There is no drop of wrath in that cup thou art called upon to drink. "I do believe," says Lady Powerscourt, "He has purchased these afflictions for us as well as everything else. Blessed be His name, it is part of His covenant to visit us with the rod." What says our Adorable Lord Himself? The words were spoken, not when He was on earth, a sojourner in a sorrowing world, but when enthroned amid the glories of Heaven: "*As many as I* LOVE, *I rebuke and chasten*" (Rev. iii. 19).

Believer! rejoice in the thought, that the rod, the chastening rod, is in the

B

hands of the living, loving Saviour,
who died for thee. Tribulation is the
King's highway, and yet that highway
is paved with love. As some flowers
before shedding their fragrance require
to be pressed, so does thy God see
meet to bruise thee. As some birds are
said to sing their sweetest notes when
the thorn pierces their bosom, so does
He appoint affliction to lacerate, that
thou mayest be driven to the wing,
singing, in thy upward soaring, *"My
heart is fixed, O God, my heart is fixed!"*
"Those," says the heavenly Leighton,
"He means to make the most resplen-
dent, He hath oftenest His tools upon."
"Our troubles," says another, "seem in
His Word to be ever in His mind. Perhaps half the commands and half the
promises He gives us there, are given
us as *troubled* men." "Were it not for
trouble," said Bickersteth, on his death-
bed, "I should not have known half of
what I know now, of the mercy, faith-

fulness, and overruling Providence of God."

Be it ours to say, Lord, I will love Thee, not only despite of Thy rod, but because of Thy rod. I will rush into the very arms that are chastising me. When Thy voice calls, as to Abraham of old, to prepare for bitter trial, be it mine to respond with bounding heart, *"Here am I !"*—and to read in the Bow which spans my darkest cloud, '*He chastens* BECAUSE *He loves.*'

"AND IT SHALL COME TO PASS,
WHEN I BRING A CLOUD OVER THE EARTH, THAT
THE BOW SHALL BE SEEN IN THE CLOUD."

"I do set this Bow in the Cloud"—

"I am the Lord, I change not; therefore ye sons of Jacob are not consumed."—Mal. iii. 6.

Immutability. THE *Unchangeableness of God.* What an anchor for the storm-tossed! "Change is our portion here." Scenes are altering. Joys are fading. Friends: some of them are removed to a distance—others have gone to the longest home of all. Who, amid these chequered experiences, does not sigh for something permanent —stable—enduring? The vessel has again and again slipped its earthly moorings. We long for some secure and sheltered harbour.

"I change not!" Heart and flesh may faint—yea, *do* faint and fail—but there is an unfainting, unfailing, unvarying God. All the changes in the world around cannot affect Him. Our own fitfulness cannot alter Him. When we are depressed, downcast, fluctuating, our treacherous hearts turning aside "like a broken bow"—*He* is without one "shadow of turning." "*God who cannot lie,*" is the superscription on His eternal throne ; and inscribed on all His dealings.

"*I change not!*" For whom does He span the darkened sky with this Bow of comfort? It is for "THE SONS OF JACOB," His own covenant people. Those clothed like Jacob of old, in the garment of the true Elder Brother, through whom they have obtained their spiritual inheritance.

Precious name! It forms a blessed guarantee that nothing can befal me but what is for my good. I cannot doubt His faithfulness. I dare not arraign the rectitude of His dispensations. It is covenant love which is now darkening my earthly horizon. This hour He is the same as when He "*spared not His own Son!*" Oh, instead of wondering at my trials, let me rather wonder that He has borne with me so long. It is of the Lord's unchanging *mercies* that I am not consumed. Had He been *man*, changeful, vacillating, as myself, long ere now would He have spurned me away, and consigned me to the doom of the cumberer. But, "*My thoughts are not your thoughts—neither are your ways my ways, saith the Lord.*" He is without any variableness. Yes, in this dark and cloudy day, I will lift up mine eyes to the covenant token, and sing through my tears, "*Happy is he that hath* THE GOD OF JACOB *for his help—whose hope is in the Lord his God!*"

"AND IT SHALL COME TO PASS,
WHEN I BRING A CLOUD OVER THE EARTH, THAT
THE BOW SHALL BE SEEN IN THE CLOUD."

"I do set this Bow in the Cloud "—
"I know their sorrows."—EXOD. iii. 7.

MAN cannot say so. There
Divine   are many sensitive fibres in
Sympathy. the soul which the best and
tenderest *human* sympathy cannot touch.
But the PRINCE OF SUFFERERS, He
who led the way in the path of sorrow,
" knoweth our frame." When crushing
bereavement lies like ice on the heart—
when the dearest earthly friend cannot
enter into the peculiarities of our grief,
JESUS *can*, Jesus *does !* He who once
bore my *sins* also carried my *sorrows.*
That eye, now on the throne, was once
dim with weeping. I can think, in all
my afflictions, " He was afflicted ; " in
all my tears, " JESUS WEPT ! "

Israel had long groaned under bond-
age. God appeared not to " know " it.
He seemed, like Baal, " asleep ; " yet
at that very moment was His pitying

eye wistfully beholding His enslaved people. It was *then* He said, " *I* KNOW *their sorrows !*"

He may *seem* at times thus to forget and forsake us ;—leaving us to utter the plaintive cry, "Hath God forgotten to be gracious ?" when all the while He is bending over us in tenderest love. He often suffers our needs to attain their extremity—that He may stretch forth His succouring hand, and reveal the plenitude of His Grace. " *Ye have seen the end of the Lord, that the Lord is very pitiful and of tender mercy*" (James v. 11).

And " knowing" our sorrows, is a blessed guarantee that none will be sent but what He sees to be needful. "I will not," says He, " make a full end of thee, but *I will correct thee* IN MEA- SURE" (Jer. xxx. 11). All He sends is precisely meted out—wisely appor- tioned. There is nothing accidental or fortuitous ;—no redundant thorn—

no superfluous pang. He "*putteth our tears into His bottle*" (Ps. lvi. 8). Each one is *counted*—drop by drop—tear by tear;—they are sacred things among the treasures of GOD. "I am detained," said one, in the midst of prolonged pain and sickness, "to learn more and more of my Saviour's love to me, and *the fellowship of His sufferings*. It may enhance my happiness, perhaps, to all eternity" (*Victory Won*).

Tried believer, the iron may have entered deeply into thy soul; yet rejoice! Great is thine honour, thus to be, in any feeble measure, identified with the sufferings of "the Man of Sorrows." Look upwards to this bright Bow encircling thy dark sky. JESUS, a sympathising Jesus, "knows" thine aching pangs and burning tears, and He will, in His own good time and in His own good way, "*come down to deliver thee.*"

"AND IT SHALL COME TO PASS, WHEN I BRING A CLOUD OVER THE EARTH, THAT THE BOW SHALL BE SEEN IN THE CLOUD."

"I do set this Bow in the Cloud "—

"If need be."—1 PET. i. 6.

A Gracious Condition. WHAT a blessed motto and superscription over the dark lintels of sorrow,—" IF NEED BE ! " Every arrow from the quiver of God is feathered with it. Write it,— Child of affliction, over every trial thy God sees meet to send ! If He calls thee down from the sunny mountain-heights to the darksome glades, hear Him saying, " *There is a need be.*" If He have dashed the cup of earthly prosperity from thy lips, curtailed thy creature comforts, diminished thy " basket and thy store," hear Him saying, " *There is a need be.*" If He has ploughed and furrowed thy soul with severe bereavement—extinguished light after light in thy dwelling—hear Him thus stilling the tumult of thy grief—" *There is a need be.*"

Yes, believe it, there is some profound

reason for thy trial, which at present
may be undiscernible. No furnace will be
hotter than He sees to be needed. Sometimes, indeed, His teachings are mysterious. We can with difficulty spell out the
letters, " *God is love:*" we can see no
"bright light"—no luminous Bow in
our Cloud. It is all mystery ; not one
break is there in the sky. Nay ! "Hear
what God the Lord doth speak "—
" *If need be.*" He does not long leave
His people alone, if He sees the chariot-
wheels dragging heavily. He will take
His own means to sever them from an
absorbing love of the world—to pursue
them out of self—and dislodge usurping
clay-idols that may have vaulted on the
throne which He alone may occupy.
Before thy present trial, He may have
seen thy love waxing cold—thy influence
for good lessening. As the sun puts out
the fire, the sun of earthly prosperity
may have been extinguishing the fires of
thy soul ;—thou mayest have been shin-

ing less brightly for Christ—effecting some guilty compromise with an insinuating and seductive world. He has appointed the very discipline and dealing needful ;—nothing *else*—nothing *less* could have done.

Be still, and know that He is God. That "need be," remember, is in the hands of Infinite *Love*, Infinite *Wisdom*, Infinite *Power*. Trust Him in *little* things as well as in *great* things—in trifles as well as in emergencies. Seek to have an unquestioning faith. Though other paths, doubtless, would have been selected by you had the choice been in your hands, be it yours to listen to His voice at every turn of the road, saying, "THIS *is the way, walk ye in it.*"

We may not be able to understand it now,—but one day we shall come to find, that AFFLICTION is one of God's most blessed angels ; — a ministering spirit, "sent forth to minister to them who are heirs of salvation." There

would be no Bow in the material
heaven but for the Cloud. Lovelier,
indeed, to the eye is the azure blue—
the fleecy summer vapours—or the gold
and vermilion of western sunsets. But
what would become of the earth if no
dark clouds from time to time hung over
it; distilling their treasures—reviving
and refreshing its drooping vegetable
tribes?

Is it otherwise with the soul? Nay.
The cloud of sorrow is *needed.* Its
every rain-drop has an inner meaning
of LOVE. If, even now, afflicted one,
these clouds are gathering, and the tempest sighing,—lift up thine eye to the
divine scroll gleaming in the darkened
heavens, and remember that He who has
put the Bow of Promise there, saw also
a *"need be"* for the cloud on which it
rests.

" AND IT SHALL COME TO PASS,
WHEN I BRING A CLOUD OVER THE EARTH, THAT
THE BOW SHALL BE SEEN IN THE CLOUD."

"I do set this Bow in the Cloud"—

"My presence shall go with thee, and I will give thee rest."—EXOD. xxxiii. 14.

Presence and Rest. MOSES asked to be shown "the way." Here is the answer :—The way is *not* shown—but better than this, God says "Trust Me"—" I will go with thee!"

Afflicted one, hear the voice addressing thee from the cloudy pillar. It is a wilderness promise which "the God of Jeshurun" speaks to His spiritual Israel still. He who led His people of old "like a flock by the hand of Moses and Aaron," will manifest towards thee the same Shepherd-love. The way may be very different from what we could have wished ;—what we *would* have chosen. But the choice is in better hands. He has His own wise and righteous ends in every devious turning in it.

Who can look back on the past lead-ings of God without gratitude and thankfulness? When His sheep have been conducted to the rougher parts of the wilderness, He, their Shepherd, has " gone before them." When their fleeces were torn, and they foot-sore and weary, —He has borne them in His arms. His presence has lightened every cross and sweetened every care. Let us trust Him for an unknown and chequered future. Other companionships we cherished may have failed us, but ONE who is better than the best, goes before us in His gracious Pillar-cloud. With Him for our portion, take what He will away, we must be happy; we can rise above the loss of the earthly gift, in the consciousness of the nobler possession and heritage we enjoy in the Great Bestower. He may have seen meet to level clay-idols, that He, the All - Satisfying, might reign paramount and supreme. He may have seen meet to take earthly " presences " away, to give us more of

His own, and to lead us to breathe more earnestly the prayer, "If THY presence go not with us, carry us not hence." He will not suffer us to rear tabernacles on earth, and to write upon them, "*This is my rest.*" No, *Tenting-time here—resting-time yonder!* But 'Fear not,' He seems to say, 'thou art not left unbefriended or unsolaced on the way. Pilgrim in a pilgrim land, "My presence shall go with thee." In all thy dark and cloudy days—in thy hours of faintness and depression—in sadness and in sorrow—in loneliness and solitude—in life and in death. And when the journey is ended,—the Pillar needed no more,—"*I will give thee* REST."' The earnest of *Grace* will be followed with the fruition of GLORY.

"AND IT SHALL COME TO PASS,
WHEN I BRING A CLOUD OVER THE EARTH, THAT
THE BOW SHALL BE SEEN IN THE CLOUD."

9TH DAY.

"I do set th's Bow in the Cloud"—

'The Lord gave, and the Lord hath taken away; blessed be the name of the Lord."—Job i. 21.

The Giver and Taker. NOBLE posture this; to kneel and to adore! To see no hand but ONE. Sabeans——Fire——Whirlwind——Sword—— are all overlooked. The Patriarch recognises alone, "THE LORD" who *gave* and "THE LORD" who had *taken.*

What is the cause of so much depression, overmuch sorrow, ungospel murmuring in our hours of trial? It is what Rutherford calls "Our looking to the confused rollings of the wheels of second causes;" a refusal to rise to 'the height of the great argument,' and confidingly to say, "*The will of* THE LORD *be done:*"—a refusal to hear His voice —His own loving voice, mingling with the accents of the rudest storm—"IT IS I!"

"*Is there evil in a city, and* THE LORD

C

hath not done it?" Is there a bitter drop in the cup, and THE LORD hath not mingled it? He loves His people too well to intrust their interests to any other. We are but clay in the hand of the Potter—vessels in the hand of the Refiner of silver. He metes out our portion. He appoints the bounds of our habitation. "*The Lord God prepared the* GOURD." "*The Lord God prepared the* WORM." He is the Author alike of mercies and sorrows, of comforts and crosses. He breathes into our nostrils the breath of life; and it is at His summons the spirit returns "to the God *who gave it.*"

Oh, that we would seek ever to regard our own lives and the lives of those dear to us as a *loan :*—God, as the Great Proprietor—who, when He sees meet, can revoke the grant or curtail the lease. "HE GAVE!" All the mercies we have are *lent* mercies ;—by Him bestowed ;—by Him continued ;—by Him withheld.

And how often does He take away,
that He may Himself enter the vacuum
of the heart and fill it with His own in-
effable presence and love! No loss can
compensate for the want of *Him;* but
He can compensate for all losses. Let
us trust His love and faithfulness as a
taking as well as a *giving* God. Often
are sense and sight tempted to say,
"Not so, Lord!" But Faith, resting
on the promise, can exult in this Bow
spanning the darkest cloud—"*Even so,
Father,* FOR SO IT SEEMS GOOD IN THY
SIGHT."

"AND IT SHALL COME TO PASS,
WHEN I BRING A CLOUD OVER THE EARTH, THAT
THE BOW SHALL BE SEEN IN THE CLOUD."

10TH DAY

"I do set this Bow in the Cloud"—

"Call upon me in the day of trouble: I will deliver thee, and thou shalt glorify me."—Ps. l. 15.

Deliverance in Trouble. How varied are our days of trouble! *Sickness*, with its hours of restlessness and languor. *Bereavement*, with its rifled treasures and aching hearts. *Loss of substance*—the curtailment or forfeiture of worldly possessions—riches taking to themselves wings and fleeing away! Or, severer than all, the woundings of friends;—abused confidence—withered affections — hopes scattered like the leaves of autumn!

But, "GOD is our refuge and strength, a very present help in trouble." Tried one, He leaves not thy defenceless head unsheltered in the storm. "*Call upon* ME." He invites thee into the pavilion of His own presence. Better the bitter Marah waters with his healing, than the purest fountain of the world and *no*

God. Better the hottest furnace flames, with One there "like the Son of God," than that the dross should be suffered to accumulate, and the soul left to cleave to the dust. He, "the Purifier of silver," is seated by these flames tempering their fury: Yea, He gives the special promise, "*I will deliver thee.*" It may not be the deliverance we expect; the deliverance we have prayed for; the deliverance we could have wished. But shall not the sorest trial be well worth enduring, if this be the result of His chastening love—"*Thou shalt glorify me*"? "*Glorify* HIM!" How? By a simple unreasoning faith—by meek, lowly, unmurmuring acquiescence in H s dealings;—these dealings endearing the Saviour and His grace more than ever to our hearts.

The Day of trouble led His saints in all ages thus to glorify Him. *David* never could have written his touching Psalms, nor *Paul* his precious Epistles, had not God cast them both into the crucible. To be the teachers of the Church of the future, they had to graduate in the school of affliction. If He be appointing us similar discipline, let it be our endeavour to glorify Him by active obedience, as well as by passive resignation ; not abandoning ourselves to selfish, moody, sentimental grief; but rather going forth on our great mission—our work and warfare—with a vaster estimate of the value of time, and the grandeur of existence.

"Give glory to the Lord your God before He cause darkness ; and before your feet stumble upon the dark mountains; and, while ye look for light, He turn it into the shadow of death, and make it gross darkness !"

"AND IT SHALL COME TO PASS,
WHEN I BRING A CLOUD OVER THE EARTH, THAT
THE BOW SHALL BE SEEN IN THE CLOUD."

"I do set this Bow in the Cloud"—

"Like as a father pitieth his children, so the Lord pitieth them that fear him."—Ps. ciii. 13.

Pitying Love. ' ABBA, FATHER !" is a Gospel word.—A Father bending over the sick-bed of his weak or dying child ;—a Mother pressing, in tender solicitude, an infant sufferer to her bosom ;—These are the earthly pictures of GOD. *"Like as a father pitieth."* *" As one whom his mother comforteth so will I comfort you."*

When tempted in our season of overwhelming sorrow to say, 'Never has there been so dark a cloud, never a heart so stript and desolate as mine,' let this thought hush every murmur, *" It is your* FATHER's *good pleasure !"* The love and pity of the tenderest earthly parent is but a dim shadow, compared to the pitying love of God. If your heavenly Father's smile has for the moment been exchanged for the chastening rod ; be assured there is some deep necessity for the altered discipline. If there be un-utterable yearnings in the soul of the earthly Parent as the lancet is applied to the body of his child,—infinitely more is it so with your covenant God, as He subjects you to these deep woundings of heart. Finite wisdom has no place in His ordinations. An earthly father *may* err—is ever erring; but "*as for God, His way is perfect.*" This is the explanation of His every dealing— "*Your heavenly Father knoweth ye have need of all these things!*"

Trust Him, when you cannot trace Him. Do not try to penetrate the cloud which *He* "brings over the earth," and to look through it. Keep your eye steadily fixed on the Bow. The mystery is God's, the Promise is yours. Seek that the end of all His dispensations may be to make you more confiding. Without one misgiving commit your way to Him. He says regarding each child of His covenant family, what He said of Ephraim of old (and never more so than in a season of suffering) —"*I do earnestly remember him still.*" Whilst now bending your head like a bulrush—your heart breaking with sorrow—remember His pitying eye is upon you. Be it yours, even through blinding tears, to say, "*Even so*, FATHER!"

"AND IT SHALL COME TO PASS,
WHEN I BRING A CLOUD OVER THE EARTH, THAT
THE BOW SHALL BE SEEN IN THE CLOUD."

"I do set this Bow in the Cloud"—

"That blessed hope, and the glorious appearing of the great God and our Saviour Jesus Christ."—TIT. ii. 13.

The Blessed Hope.

WHAT a bright Bow for a storm - wreathed sky! HOPE is a joyous emotion. Poetry sings of it; Music warbles its lofty aspirations; but alas! how often does it weave fantastic visions—give birth to shadowy dreams, which appear, and then vanish. "In the morning" the flowers of life are flourishing and growing up;—"In the evening" a mysterious blight comes—they lie withered garlands at our feet. The longing aspirations of a whole lifetime seem realised;—one wave of calamity overtakes us, and washes all away.

BUT, there is *one* "Blessed Hope" beyond the possibility of blight or decay—"The hope of the glory of God," the hope "which maketh not ashamed" —"the glorious appearing of the Great God our Saviour."

If we long, on earth, for the return of an absent friend or brother, separated from us for a season, by intervening oceans or continents;—if we count the weeks or months, till we can welcome him back again to the parental home,—how should the Christian long for the return of the "*Brother of brothers*," the Friend of friends?   "I will come again," is His own gracious promise, "to receive you unto myself."

Oh, happy day! when He shall be "glorified in His saints;"—when His people will suffer no more, and sin no more. No more couches of sickness, or aching heads—or fevered brows; no more opened graves, or bitter tears;—and, better than all, no more guilty estrangements and traitor unholy hearts. It will be the bridal day of the soul. The body slumbering in the dust will be reunited, a glorified body, to the redeemed spirit. The grave shall be for ever spoiled—death swallowed up in eternal victory. "So shall we *ever* be with the Lord!"

Reader, dost thou "love His appearing"? Art thou in the eager expectant attitude of those who are "*looking for, and hasting unto the coming of the day of God*"? "Yet a little while, and He that shall come, will come." If thou art a child of the covenant, having conscious filial nearness to the Throne of *grace*, thou needest not dread the Throne of *glory*. True, He is the "great God," but He is "*our Saviour*." It is a "Kinsman Redeemer" who is ordained "to judge the world in righteousness." Yes, turn thine eye ofttimes towards this bright Bow spanning a glorious future—for remember, it is "to them who LOOK for Him," that He shall "appear the second time, without sin, unto salvation."

"AND IT SHALL COME TO PASS,
WHEN I BRING A CLOUD OVER THE EARTH, THAT
THE BOW SHALL BE SEEN IN THE CLOUD."

"I do set this Bow in the Cloud"—

'The righteous is taken away from the evil to come. He shall enter into peace! They shall rest in their beds."
—ISA. lvii. 1, 2.

A Gracious Removal. How this thought reconciles to earth's saddest separations! The early (what we are apt to think the *too* early) graves of our "loved and lost," have saved them much sorrow, much suffering, much *sin!* Who can tell what may have been brooding in a dark horizon? The fairest vessel—the life freighted with greatest promise—might have made shipwreck in this world's treacherous sea. My God knows what was best. If He plucked His lily soon, it was to save it some rough blast. If He early folded His lamb, it was to save it having its fleece soiled with earthly corruption. If the port of glory was soon entered, it was because He foresaw threatening tempests that were screened from our limited vision—"*So*

He brought them to the haven where they would be ! "

Yes, *the quiet haven.* The storms of life are over. That shore is undisturbed by one murmuring wave. "He shall enter" (he *has* entered) "into peace:"—the rest which " *remaineth.*" Did the ransomed dead, at the hour of their departure, sink into blank oblivion —inherit only everlasting silence,—sad indeed would be the pang of separation. But, " Weep not ! she is not dead, but *sleepeth.*" Yea, weep not ! She is not dead, but *liveth !* At the very moment earth's tears are falling, the spirit is sunning in the realms of everlasting day, safely housed, safely *Home.* The body "rests in its bed." The grave is its couch of repose. We bid it the long "good night" in the joyful expectancy of a glorious re-union at the waking - time of immortality — that " morning without clouds," whose " sun shall no more go down."

Child of sorrow, mourning over the withdrawal of some beloved object of earthly affection. Dry thy tears · An early death has been an early crown. The tie sundered here, links thee to the throne of God. Thou hast a brother, a sister, a child, in Heaven. Thou art the relative of a ransomed saint. We are proud when we hear of our friends being "advanced" in this world. What are the world's noblest promotions, in comparison with that of the believer at death, when he graduates from grace to glory? when he exchanges the pilgrim warfare for the eternal rest?

Often, in thine hours of sadness, contrast the *certainty* of present bliss, with the *possibilities* of a suffering, sorrowing, sinning future,—the joys in possession, with the evils which *might* have been in reversion. Thou mayst now, like the Shunammite of old, be gazing with tearful eye on some withered blossom ; but when the question is put, " *Is it well with thee? Is it well with thy husband? Is it well with the child?"* in the elevating confidence that they have "entered into peace," and are "resting in their beds," be it thine, joyfully to answer, "*It* is *well!*"

"AND IT SHALL COME TO PASS,
WHEN I BRING A CLOUD OVER THE EARTH, THAT
THE BOW SHALL BE SEEN IN THE CLOUD."

"I do set this Bow in the Cloud"—

" What I do, thou knowest not now ; but thou shalt
know hereafter."—JOHN xii. 7.

Unveiled Mysteries. MUCH is baffling
and perplexing to
us in God's present dealings. " What!"
we are often ready to exclaim, " could
not the cup have been less bitter—the
trial less severe—the road less rough
and dreary ? " " Hush thy misgivings,"
says a gracious God ; "arraign not the
rectitude of My dispensations. Thou
shalt yet see all revealed and made
bright in the mirror of eternity."

" What *I* do!"—it is all *My* doing—*My*
appointment. *Thou* hast but a partial
view of these dealings ;—they are seen,
by the eye of sense, through a dim and
distorted medium. *Thou* canst see nought
but plans crossed, and gourds laid low,
and 'beautiful rods' broken. But, *I* see
the end from the beginning. "Shall not
the Judge of all the earth do right ? "

D

And "*Thou* SHALT *know*." Wait for
the "hereafter" revelation. An earthly
father puzzles not the ear of infancy
with hard sayings and involved prob-
lems. He waits for a more advanced
stage of existence, and then unfolds all.
So it is with God. *We* are now in our
nonage ;—children lisping in infancy a
knowledge of His ways. We shall learn
"the deep things of God" in the man-
hood of eternity. Christ now often
shews Himself only "behind the lat-
tice,"—a glimpse and He is gone. But
the day is coming when we shall "see
Him as He is:"—when every dark
hieroglyphic in the Roll of Providence
will be interpreted and expounded.

It is unfair to criticise the half-finished
picture—to censure or condemn the half-
developed plan. God's plans are here
in embryo. "We see," says Rutherford, "but broken links of the chains
of His Providence. Let the former
work His own clay in what frame

He pleaseth." But a flood of light will break upon us from the Sapphire Throne—"In Thy light, we shall see light." The "need be," muffled as a secret now, will be confided to us *then*, and become luminous with love.

Perhaps we may not even have to wait till Eternity, for the realisation of this promise. We may experience its fulfilment here. We not unfrequently find, even in this present world, mysterious dispensations issuing in unlooked-for blessing. *Jacob* would never have seen *Joseph* had he not parted with *Benjamin*. Often would the believer never have seen *the true* JOSEPH had he not been called on to part with his best beloved. His language, at the time, is that of the Patriarch—"I *am indeed bereaved.*" "*All these things are against me!*" But the things which he imagined to be so adverse, have proved the means of leading him to see the heavenly King "in his beauty" before he dies. Much is sent

to "humble us and to prove us." It
may not do us good *now*, but it is promised to do so "*at the latter end.*"

I shall not dictate to my God what
His ways *should* be.   The patient does
not dictate to his Physician.   He does
not reject and refuse the prescription
because it is nauseous;—He knows it
is for his good, and takes it on trust.   It
is for faith to repose in whatever God
appoints.   Let me not wrong His love
or dishonour His faithfulness, by sup-
posing that there is one needless or redundant drop in the cup which His
loving wisdom has mingled.   "*Now we
know in part, but* THEN *shall we know
even as also we are known !*"

"AND IT SHALL COME TO PASS,
WHEN I BRING A CLOUD OVER THE EARTH, THAT
THE BOW SHALL BE SEEN IN THE CLOUD."

"I do set this Bow in the Cloud"—

"I have chosen thee in the furnace of affliction."
—ISA. xlviii. 10.

The Choosing Place. THE FURNACE OF AF-
FLICTION. It is God's
meeting-place with His
people. '"I have chosen thee," says
He, there; I will keep thee there, till
the purifying process is complete; and,
if need be, in a "chariot of FIRE" I
will carry thee to heaven!' Some Fires
are for destruction, but this is for puri-
fication. He, the *Refiner*, is sitting by
the furnace, regulating the flames, tempering the heat; not the least filing of
the gold but what is precious to Him.
The bush is burning with *fire*, but He is
in the midst of it;—a living God in the
bush—a living Saviour in the furnace!

And has not this been the method
of His dealing with His faithful people
in every age. First, trial; then, blessings. First, straits; then, deliverances:

Egypt—plagues—darkness—brickkilns—the Red Sea—forty years of desert privations—THEN *Canaan*. First, the burning fiery furnace; then, the vision of "one like the Son of God!" Or, as with Elijah on Carmel, the answer is first by *fire*, and then by *rain*. First, the fiery trial, then the gentle descent of the Spirit's influences, coming down "like rain upon the mown grass, and as showers that water the earth."

Believer, be it yours to ask, Are my trials sanctified? Are they making me holier, purer, better; more meek, more gentle, more heavenly-minded, more Saviour-like? Seek to "*glorify God in the fires.*" Patience is a grace which the Angels cannot manifest. It is a flower of earth;—it blooms not in Paradise; it requires tribulation for its exercise; it is nurtured only amid wind, and hail, and storm. Remember, by patient, unmurmuring submission, you, a poor sinner, can thus magnify your

God in a way the loftiest angelic natures cannot do! He is taking you to the inner chambers of His covenant faithfulness. His design is to purge away your dross, to bring you forth from the furnace reflecting His own image, and fitted for glory. Those intended for great usefulness are much in the fining-pot. "His children," says Romaine, "have found suffering times happy times. They never have such nearness to their Father, such holy freedom with Him, and such heavenly refreshment with Him, as under the cross."

"Beloved, think it not strange concerning the *fiery* trial which is to try you, ... but rejoice!"

"AND IT SHALL COME TO PASS,
WHEN I BRING A CLOUD OVER THE EARTH, THAT
THE BOW SHALL BE SEEN IN THE CLOUD"

"I do set this Bow in the Cloud"—

"The days of thy mourning shall be ended."—Isa. lx. 20.

Mourning Ended. THE believer has "mourning days." The place of his sojourn is a *valley of tears.* Adam went weeping from *his* paradise, we go weeping on the way to ours. But, pilgrim of grief! thy tears are numbered. A few more aching sighs —a few more gloomy clouds—and the eternal sun shall burst on thee, whose radiance shall never more be obscured. Life may be to thee one long "Valley of Baca"—a protracted scene of "weeping:"—but soon shalt thou hear the sweet chimes wafted from the towers of the new Jerusalem, "Enter into the *joy* of thy Lord." "*The Lord God shall wipe away all tears from off all faces!*"

"*The* DAYS *of thy mourning.*" It is a consoling thought that all these days are appointed—meted out—numbered. "Unto you it is GIVEN," says

the apostle, . . " to *suffer !* " Yes, and
if thou art a child of the covenant, thy
mourning days are days of special privi-
lege, intended to be fraught with blessing. To the unbeliever, they are earnests
of everlasting woe ;—to the believer, they
are preludes and precursors of eternal
glory ! Affliction to the one is the cloud
without the Bow,—to the other, it is the
cloud radiant and lustrous with gospel
promise and gospel hope.

Reader, art thou now one of the
many members of the family of sorrow ?
Be comforted. Soon the long night-
watch will be over — pain, sickness,
weakness, weariness. Soon the win-
dows of the soul will be no more darkened. Soon thou shalt have nothing to
be delivered from,—thy present losses
and crosses will turn into eternal gains,
—the dews of the night of weeping
(nature's tear-drops) will come to sparkle
like beauteous gems in the morning of
immortality ! Soon the Master's foot-

steps will be heard, saying, "The days of thy mourning are ended," and thou shalt take off thy sackcloth, and be girded with gladness.

Up to that moment, thy life may have been one long "day" of mourning But once past the golden portals, and the eye can be dim no more ;—the very fountain of weeping will be dried! The period of your *mourning* is counted by "DAYS;"—of your eternal *rejoicing* by *eras and cycles.* "Why art thou then cast down, O my soul, and why art thou disquieted within me? Hope thou in God!" I will gaze through my tears on this celestial rainbow, and sing this "song in the night," which the God, who is to wipe my tears away, has put into my lips: "*And there shall be no more death, neither sorrow nor crying ; neither shall there be any more pain, for the former things are passed away !*"

"AND IT SHALL COME TO PASS, WHEN I BRING A CLOUD OVER THE EARTH, THAT THE BOW SHALL BE SEEN IN THE CLOUD."

"I do set this Bow in the Cloud"—

"I will never leave thee, nor forsake thee."—HEB. xiii. 5.

The Abiding Friend. No human friend can say so. The closest and dearest of earthly links may be broken, yea, *have* been broken. Distance may part—time estrange—the grave sunder. Loving earthly looks may only greet thee now in mute smiles from the portrait on the wall. But here is an unfainting, unvarying, unfailing Friend. Sorrowing one, amid the wreck of earthly joys which thou mayest be even now bewailing; here is a message sent to thee from thy God—"*I will never leave thee, nor forsake thee!*" Thy gourd has withered, but He who gave it thee remains. Surrender thyself to His disposal. He wishes to shew thee His present sufficiency for thy happiness. As ofttimes thy heart in silence and sadness weaves its plaintive lament, "Joseph is not, and Simeon is not:" think of Him who hath promised to set "the solitary in families" (Ps. lxviii. 6), and to "give unto them a name and a place better than of sons or of daughters." Alone: thou art *not* alone! Turn in self-oblivion to Jesus. It is not, it cannot be "night," if He, "the Sun of thy soul," be ever near. In the morning, He comes with the earliest beam that visits thy chamber. When the curtains of night close around thee, He, to whom "the darkness and the light are both alike," is at thy side.—In the stillness of night, when in thy wakeful moments, the visions of the departed flit before thee like shadows on the wall;—He, the unslumbering Shepherd of Israel, is tending thy couch, and whispering in thine ear, "Fear not, for *I* am with thee!"

Thy experience may be that of Paul, "All forsook me." But, like him also, thou wilt, doubtless, be able to add in the extremity of thy sorrow, "*Never-theless*, THE LORD stood with me, and strengthened me!" (2 Tim. iv. 16, 17). His favour is life. He can compensate, by His own loving presence, for every earthly loss. Without the consciousness of His friendship and love, the smallest trial will crush thee. With Him *in* thy trial, supporting and sustaining thee under it (yea, coming in the place of those thou mournest), thou wilt have an infinite and inexhaustible Portion for a finite and mutable one. Many a cloud is there without a Bow in Nature—but never in Grace. Every sorrow has its corresponding and counterpart comfort; —"*In the multitude of the* SORROWS *that I had in my heart, Thy* COMFORTS *have refreshed my soul*" (Prayer-book Version.) If, in the midnight of grief, thy earthly sun appear to have set for ever, an inner, but not less real sunshine, lights up thy stricken heart. The stream of life may have been poisoned at its source; but blessed be His name, if it have driven thee to say, "All my springs are IN THEE." "The LORD is my portion, saith my soul, therefore will I hope in Him!"

"AND IT SHALL COME TO PASS,
WHEN I BRING A CLOUD OVER THE EARTH, THAT
THE BOW SHALL BE SEEN IN THE CLOUD."

18th Day.

"I do set this Bow in the Cloud"—

"He doth not afflict willingly, nor grieve the children
of men."—LAM. iii. 33.

Unwilling Discipline. In our seasons of
trial, when under
some inscrutable dispensation, how apt
is the murmuring thought to rise in our
hearts—"*All these things are against
me!*" Might not this overwhelming
blow have been spared? Might not
this dark cloud, which has shadowed
my heart and my home with sadness,
have been averted? Might not the
accompaniments of my trial have been
less severe—"*Surely the Lord hath forgotten to be gracious?*"

Nay, these afflictions are errands of
mercy in disguise—"*He afflicteth not
willingly.*" There is nothing capricious
or arbitrary about thy God's dealings.
Unutterable *tenderness* is the character-
istic of all His allotments. The world
may wound by unkindness;—trusted

friends may become treacherous;—a brother may speak with unnecessary harshness and severity; but the Lord is "abundant in goodness and in truth." He appoints no needless pang. When he appears like Joseph to "speak *roughly*," there are gentle undertones of love. The stern accents are assumed, because He has precious lessons that could not otherwise have been taught.

Ah! be assured, there is some deep *necessity* in all He does. In our calendars of sorrow we may put this luminous mark against every trying hour, "*It was needed!*" Some redundant branch in the tree required pruning. Some wheat required to be cast overboard to lighten the ship and avert further disaster. Mourning one,—He might have dealt far otherwise with thee. He might have cut thee down as a fruitless, worthless cumberer. He might have abandoned thee, to drift, disowned and unpiloted, on the rocks of destruction:—

joined to thine idols, He might have left thee " alone," to settle on thy lees, and forfeit thine eternal bliss ! But He loved thee better. It was kindness, infinite kindness, which blighted thy fairest blossoms, and hedged up thy way with thorns. "Without this hedge of thorns," says Richard Baxter, " on the right hand and on the left, we should hardly be able to keep the way to heaven."

We, in our blind unbelief, may speak of trials we imagine might have been spared—chastisements that are unnecessarily severe. But the day is coming when every step of the Lord's procedure will be vindicated ; when we shall own and recognise each separate experience of sorrow to have been an unspeakably precious and important period in the history of the soul. Yes,—child of God. The messenger of affliction has an olive-branch in one hand—a love-token plucked from the bowers of paradise—and in the other, a chalice mingled

E

by One, too loving and gracious, to in-
sert one needless ingredient of sorrow!
Remember, every drop of wrath in that
cup was exhausted by a surety-Saviour.
In taking it into thy hand, be it thine
to extract support and consolation from
what so mightily sustained a Greater
Sufferer in a more awful hour :—" *This
cup which* THOU *givest me to drink, shall
I not drink it ?*"

"AND IT SHALL COME TO PASS,
WHEN I BRING A CLOUD OVER THE EARTH, THAT
THE BOW SHALL BE SEEN IN THE CLOUD."

"I do set this Bow in the Cloud"—

" I am he that liveth, and was dead; and, behold, I am
alive for evermore, Amen; and have the keys of hell
and of death."—REV. i. 18.

Death Vanquished. AN enthroned Saviour speaks! " *I*," says He, " am he that liveth," (or, " *the Living one*.") Others have passed away; but I ever live, and ever love. I am *now* living, a personal Saviour— " Christ thy *life!* " Art thou stooping over some treasured house of clay which the whirlwind has made a mass of ruins ? *I* roused the whirlwind from its chamber. *I* appointed the startling dispensation. *I* ordered the shroud, and prepared the grave ! Let not 'accident,' 'chance,' 'fate,' enter the vocabulary of thy sorrow. I am the Lord of *death* as well as of *life*. I have the keys of " Hades and of the grave " suspended at my girdle. The tomb is never unlocked but by Me. Let others talk of

the might of the King of Terrors. He
has *no* might but by My permission.

More than this,—Mourning one, "*I
was* DEAD." I myself once entered that
gloomy portico. I sanctified and con-
secrated it by My presence. I was a
Tenant of the tomb. This now glorified
Body was once laid by human hands in
a borrowed Grave! Canst thou dread
to walk the Valley trodden by thy Lord?
—to encounter the "last enemy," which
He fought and conquered. *Death!*—it
has been converted by Him into a "pa-
renthesis in endless life."

"*I am He that was* DEAD"—"*I am
He that* LIVETH." What more could
the Christian desire than this twofold
assurance? On the Day of Atonement
of old, the blood was sprinkled alike on
the floor and on the mercy-seat;—the
voice of blood arose from the floor below,
and the mercy-seat above. So it is with
the voice of our Elder Brother's blood.
It cried first from earth beneath, and

it now cries from Heaven. His *dying* love, is ever-*living;*—imperishable and immutable as His own being!

As the Bow in the material firmament can never cease to appear, so long as the present laws of nature continue, and there is a sun in the heavens; so the Bow of the Everlasting Covenant, and all its blessings, can only fail when Christ, the Sun of Righteousness, ceases to shine, and ceases to be! With such a Bow over-arching the future,—one limb resting amid the cloudlands of life, the other melting its hues among the deeper shadows of the Valley of Death, "*I will fear no evil, for Thou,*" O SAVIOUR GOD, "*art with me, thy rod and thy staff they comfort me.*"

"AND IT SHALL COME TO PASS,
WHEN I BRING A CLOUD OVER THE EARTH, THAT
THE BOW SHALL BE SEEN IN THE CLOUD."

"I do set this Bow in the Cloud"—

" He that spared not His own Son, but delivered him up
for us all—how shall He not with him also freely
give us all things?"—ROM. viii. 32.

The
Greatest Gift.

THESE are amazing
words. God—the In-
finite God—identify-
ing Himself (so to speak) with the experiences of human sorrow;—silencing
every murmur with the unanswerable
argument—'*I* spared not *my own Son*
I gave my Greatest gift for *thee ;*—wilt
thou not cheerfully surrender thy best to
Me? Canst thou refuse, after *this* un-
speakable gift of My love, to trust Me
in lesser things? The Greater gift may
surely well be a pledge for the bestowment of all needed subordinate good.'

He promises to give " *all things ;*"—
these " all things" are in His hand.
They will be selected and allotted by
His loving wisdom ;—crosses as well as
comforts—sorrows and tears, as well as
smiles and joys. Mourning one, this

very trial which now dims thine eye is one of these " all things." Trust His faithfulness. He would as soon wound the Son of His love, as wound *thee !*

" *How shall He not give ?* " There is a " blessed impossibility," after the bestowment of *the Gift of Gifts*, that He will inflict one unnecessary trial, or withhold one needed boon. Think of His love when He offered His Isaac on the altar. It is the same at this hour—Infinite—Immutable. Yes, we may well be reconciled, even to the denial of earthly blessedness, because ordered by Him who gave *Jesus*. Lying meekly in the arms of His mercy, be it ours to say in filial confidingness—" Lord, anything with Thy love—anything *but* Thy frown !"

" *All things.*"—The *whole* range of human wants and necessities is known to Him. The care He invites me to cast upon Him is " *all* my care "—the need " *all* my need." This is His own special promise—"And God is able to make *all* grace abound toward you; that ye, always having *all sufficiency* in *all things,* may abound to every good work" (2 Cor. ix. 8). He will give me nothing and deny me nothing, but what is for my good. Let me not question the appointments of infinite wisdom. Let me not wound Him by one dishonouring doubt. Let me lean upon Him in little things as well as in great things. After the pledge of His love in *Jesus*, nothing can come wrong that comes from His hands. If tempted at times to harbour some unkind misgivings, let the sight of the cross dispel it. Looking to the Bow in the cloud gleaming with the words— *" He loved me and gave Himself for me !"* be it mine to say—

> Lord, though Thou bend my spirit low,
> Love only will I see;
> The very hand that strikes the blow,
> Was wounded once for me.

"AND IT SHALL COME TO PASS, WHEN I BRING A CLOUD OVER THE EARTH, THAT THE BOW SHALL BE SEEN IN THE CLOUD."

"I do set this Bow in the Cloud"—

"Them also which sleep in Jesus will God bring with him."—1 THESS. iv. 14.

Sleeping and
Waking.

OR, as these words have been rendered—" Them also which are *laid asleep in Jesus.*"

We bid an earthly friend " Good right" in the pleasing expectation of meeting next morning. The saints are " laid asleep" in the grave by Jesus, in the sure and certain hope of meeting Him in the morning of immortality.

Child of God, weep not for those who have " departed to be with Christ." It is with them " far better." Think not of them as " *gone.*" That is a word taken from the vocabulary of death, and which, it is to be feared, is often employed with many in the heathen sense of *annihilation.* Seek not " the living among the dead" Think rather that

the last sigh was scarce over on earth,
when the song was begun in Heaven.
The Spirit winged its arrowy flight
among ministering seraphim. Hear that
voice stealing down in the soft whisper
of Heaven's music, and saying—" *If ye
loved me ye would rejoice, because I
said, I go unto my Father !*"

The body, the casket of this immortal
jewel, is left for a season to the dis-
honours of the tomb. But it is only for
a brief " night-watch." That dust is
precious, because redeemed. Body as
well as soul was purchased by the life-
blood of Immanuel. Angels guard these
slumbering ashes ;—and the day is com
ing, when God shall " send His angels
with a great sound of a trumpet, and
they shall gather together His elect from
the four winds, from one end of Heaven
to the other." Oh, if there be " joy
among the angels of God over *one* sinner
that *repenteth*,"—what shall be the joy
of those Blessed beings over the myriads

of rising dead, hastening at their summons to their crowns and thrones !

Christian mourner, " Thy brother shall rise again." Wish him not back amid the storms of the wilderness. Be thankful rather that the wheat is no longer out in the tempest and rain ; but safely garnered—eternally housed. Thou wouldst not, surely, if thou couldst, weep that blest one from glory—ask him to unlearn Heaven's language—and be once more involved in the dust of battle ? Nay, rather " rejoice in hope of the glory of God." Death is not an eternal sleep. " Yet a little while, and He that shall come will come, and will not tarry." Jesus is now whispering in thine ear the glorious secret hid from ages and generations, and which was left to Him, as " the Abolisher of Death," to disclose : " Thy dead shall live ; together with My dead body shall they arise." He is pointing thee onward to that hour of jubilee, when the summons shall be addressed to all his sleeping saints : " *Awake and sing, ye that dwell in dust !* "

Oh happy day ! when I shall see my Saviour God in all the glories of His exalted Humanity ; and *with* Him, the once " loved and lost," now the loved and glorified, never to be lost again ! " *The Lord my God shall come, and all the saints with thee.*"—Not one shall be wanting.—In concert with those whose tongues are now silent on earth, we shall then unite in the lofty anthem, sung by the ingathered Church triumphant—" O death, where is thy sting ? O grave, where is thy victory ? Thanks be to God, who giveth us the victory through the Lord Jesus Christ."

"AND IT SHALL COME TO PASS,
WHEN I BRING A CLOUD OVER THE EARTH, THAT
THE BOW SHALL BE SEEN IN THE CLOUD."

22D DAY.

"I do set this Bow in the Cloud"—

" We know that all things work together for good to them
that love God, to them who are the called according
to his purpose."—ROM. viii. 28.

𝔈𝔫𝔟𝔦𝔰𝔦𝔟𝔩𝔢 WE are apt to " limit the
𝔥𝔞𝔯𝔪𝔬𝔫𝔦𝔢𝔰. Holy One of Israel," and
to say, 'Some things have
worked together for our good.' God
says, " All things ! " Joys, sorrows,
crosses, losses, prosperity, adversity,
health, sickness ; the gourd bestowed,
and the gourd withered ; the cup full,
and the cup emptied ; the lingering
sick-bed, the early grave !

Often, indeed, would sight and sense
lead us to doubt the reality of the promise. We can see, in many things,
scarce a dim reflection of love. Useful lives taken,—blossoms prematurely
plucked,—spiritual props removed,—
benevolent schemes blown upon. But
the apostle does not say, " We SEE,"
but " We KNOW." It is the province

of faith to trust God in the dark. The uninitiated and undiscerning cannot understand or explain the revolutions and dependencies of the varied wheels in a complicated machine; but they have confidence in the wisdom of the Artificer, that all is designed to "work out" some great and useful end.

Be it ours to write over every mysterious dealing, "*This also cometh from the Lord of hosts, who is wonderful in counsel and excellent in working.*" Let us be still and know that He is God. "We have a wonderful advertisement of a Physician from the Spirit of Truth," says Lady Powerscourt, "*who healeth* ALL *thy diseases.*" . . . . "We require but one thing, to take *all* He has prescribed, bitter as well as sweet." He will yet vindicate His own rectitude and faithfulness in our trials; our own souls will be made the better for them; He himself will be glorified *in* them. ' Doubt not my love,' He seems to say :

' the day is coming when you shall have all mysteries explained, all secrets unravelled ; and this very trial demonstrated to be *one* of the " all things " working together for your good.' " Men see not the bright light in the clouds ;" " but it shall come to pass that *at* EVENING TIME *it shall be* LIGHT ! "

"AND IT SHALL COME TO PASS,
WHEN I BRING A CLOUD OVER THE EARTH, THAT
THE BOW SHALL BE SEEN IN THE CLOUD."

"I do set this Bow in the Cloud"—

"Jesus Christ, the same yesterday, and to-day, and for
ever."—Heb. xiii. 8.

The Unchanging Name. ALL is changing here. Life is a kaleidoscope, made up of shifting forms ;—new scenes, new tastes, new feelings, new associations ;—an alternation of cloud and sunshine, tempest and calm. Its joys are like the airy bubbles on the stream, tinted with sunlight : we touch them—they are gone ! We have to tell of vacant seats in our sanctuaries —vacant seats at our home-hearths— the music of well-known voices hushed. Often, just when we imagine we have at last obtained a stable footing, the scaffolding gives way, the prop on which for a lifetime we had been leaning fails and we feel ourselves out amid the pitiless storm.

But is there nothing stable amid all this mutability ?—nothing secure and

abiding amid these fleeting shadows?
Yes, JESUS is without *any* variableness.
Eighteen hundred years have rolled by
since He left our world. The world
has changed, but He is to this hour the
same. We can follow Him through all
His wondrous pilgrimage of love on
earth. We can behold *Penitence* crouch-
ing at His feet, and sent away for-
given ;—*Sorrow* tracking His footsteps
with tears, and sent away with her tears
dried and her wounded spirit healed;—
Pain and *Sickness*, pleading with pallid
lip and wasted feature ;—and *Disease*,
at His omnipotent mandate, taking
wings to itself and fleeing away. And
He who is now on the Heavenly Throne
is " *that same Jesus.*" His ascension-
glories have not changed His changeless
heart, or alienated His affections. In
Him we have a Rock, which the billows
of adversity cannot shake. The spent
fury of the chafing waves may reach
us,—no more ; and this only endearing

F

the security and value of the *abiding
Refuge*!

How often does God rouse the storm
to drive us from all creature confidences
to the only stable One. How often does
He poison and pollute the stream to
lead us to seek the everlasting Fountain-head. We may have lost much;
but if we have found Thee, O blessed
Saviour, we possess infinitely more than
we have forfeited. We can glory in the
persuasion that nothing can ever separate us from Thy love. Our best earthly
friends; a look may alienate;—an unin-
tentional word may estrange,—the Grave
must sunder. But "*the* Lord *liveth,
and blessed be my Rock, and let the
God of my salvation be exalted.*" What
Thou hast been "yesterday"—yea, from
everlasting ages—Thou art this day, and
Thou *shalt* be for ever and ever! We
can look to the Bow of thy promises and
behold all of them in Thee "*yea* and
amen." Thou art addressing us from

Thy Throne in glory—that Throne spoken
of in Revelation as encircled with "the
rainbow of emerald" (the emblem of *per-
petuity*), and saying, "Fear not, I am
He that liveth and was dead, and behold I am alive for evermore." "Because I live, ye shall live also."

"AND IT SHALL COME TO PASS,
WHEN I BRING A CLOUD OVER THE EARTH, THAT
THE BOW SHALL BE SEEN IN THE CLOUD."

"I do set this Bow in the Cloud"—

" As thy days, so shall thy strength be."—
DEUT. xxxiii. 25.

Strength for
the Day.

BELIEVER! hast thou not
felt it so? Hast thou not
found plants distilling
balm, growing beside sorrow's path?
—succours and supports vouchsafed,
which were undreamt of till the dreaded
cloud had burst, and the day of trial
had come? Trouble not thyself regarding an unknown and veiled future; but
cast *all* thy cares on God. " Our
sandals," says a saint now in glory,
" are proof against the roughest path."
He whose name is " the God of all
grace" is better than His word. He
will be found equal to all the emergencies of His people—enough for each
moment and each hour as they come.
He never takes us to the bitter Marah
streams, but He reveals also the hidden
branch. Paul was hurled down from

the third heavens to endure the smarting of His " thorn," but he rises like a giant from his fall, exulting in the sustaining grace of an " all-sufficient God."

The beautiful peculiarity in this promise is, that God proportions His grace to the nature and the season of trial. He does not forestal or advance a supply of grace, but when the needed season and exigency comes, then the appropriate strength and support are imparted. He does not send the Bow *before* the cloud, but when the cloud appears, the Bow is seen in it. He gives sustaining grace for a trying day, and dying grace for a dying day.

Reader, do not morbidly brood on the future. Live on the promise. When the morrow comes with its trials, Jesus will come with the morrow, and with its trials too. Present grace is enough for present necessity. Trust God for the future. We honour Him, not by anticipating trial, but by confiding in His faithfulness, and crediting His assurance, that no temptation will be sent greater than we are able to bear. Even if you should see fresh clouds returning after the rain, be ready to say—" *I will fear no evil, for* THOU *art with me!* "

Insufficient you are of yourself for any trial—but " your sufficiency is of God." The promise is not " *Thy* grace," but " *My* grace is sufficient." Oh, trust His " all-sufficiency in all things." JEHOVAH-JIREH, " *the Lord will provide.* " See written over every trying hour of the future, " So *shall thy strength be!* "

" AND IT SHALL COME TO PASS,
WHEN I BRING A CLOUD OVER THE EARTH, THAT
THE BOW SHALL BE SEEN IN THE CLOUD."

25TH DAY.

"I do set this Bow in the Cloud"—

' I will ransom them from the power of the grave : I will
redeem them from death : O Death, I will be thy
plagues : O Grave, I will be thy destruction.'—
Hos. xiii. 14.

The Grave Spoiled. CHRISTIAN! the Grave is lighted with Immanuel's love. The darkest of all clouds, that which rests over the realms of Death, has the brightest Bow in it. These gloomy portals are not to hold the ruined framework for ever. The land of forgetfulness, where thy buried treasure lies, is not a winter of unbroken darkness and desolation. A glorious spring-time of revival is promised, when the mortal shall put on immortality, and the corruptible shall be clothed with " incorruption."

The Resurrection of the body. It is the climax of the work of Jesus—its culminating glory. St Paul represents a longing Church—as " waiting for the adoption (to wit), *the redemption of the*

body." It was the pre-eminent theme
of his preaching, "He preached unto
them Jesus, *and the resurrection of the
dead.*" It was the loved article in his
creed, which engrossed his own holiest
aspirations, "If by any means I might
attain unto *the resurrection of the
dead.*" It was the grand solace he ad-
ministered to other mourners.   It is
not when speaking of the immediate
bliss of the departed *spirit* at the hour
of death;—but it is when dwelling on
"the last trump"—the dead "rising in-
corruptible," and "caught up," in their
resurrection bodies, "to meet the Lord,"
that he says—" *Wherefore comfort one
another with these words.*"

Blessed day—the great Easter of
creation; the dawn of the Sabbatic
morn; the Jubilee of a triumphant
Church! Christian mourner, go not
to the grave to *weep* there. Every
particle of that mouldering dust is redeemed by the oblation of Calvary;

and the great Abolisher of death is only
waiting the ingathering of His elect, to
give the commission to his angels regarding *all* His saints, which He gave
of old regarding *one*, " Loose him, and
let him go !"

And who can image forth the glory
of these Resurrection bodies, reunited
to their glorified companion-spirits,
fashioned like their Lord's ? every sense,
every faculty—purified, sublimated, in-
stinct with holiness ; emulous with ar-
dour in His service, eager to execute His
will ; retaining, it may be, the personal
identities of earth, the old features worn
in the " nether valley ;" now, reunited
to death-divided friends in ties which
know no dissolution ;—no trace of grief
lingering on their countenances—no
accents of sorrow trembling on their
tongues. The Lamb, in the midst of
the throne, "leading" them and "feed-
ing" them ; climbing along with them,
steep by steep, in the path of life, and

saying at each ascending step in the endless progression, "I will show you greater things than these!"

Meanwhile He has Himself risen as the pledge of this Resurrection of all His people. The Great Sheaf has been waved before the Throne, as the Earnest of the mighty Harvest. *"Christ the first fruits, afterward they that are Christ's at His coming."*

"Blessed and holy is he that hath part in the first Resurrection!"

"AND IT SHALL COME TO PASS, WHEN I BRING A CLOUD OVER THE EARTH, THAT THE BOW SHALL BE SEEN IN THE CLOUD."

26TH DAY.

"I do set this Bow in the Cloud"—

" I have loved thee with an everlasting love ; therefore with loving-kindness have I drawn thee !"—JER. xxxi. 3.

Everlasting Love. BELIEVER, art thou tempted now to doubt His love ? Are His footsteps lost amid the night shadows through which He is now conducting thee ? Remember He had His eye upon thee before the birth of time ; yea, from all eternity. What appears to thee now, some sudden capricious exercise of His power or sovereignty, is the determination and decree of " everlasting love." ' I loved thee,' He seems to say, ' Suffering one, *into* this affliction ; I will love thee *through* it ; and when My designs regarding thee are completed, I will show thee that the love which is *from* everlasting, is *to* everlasting !'

Child of God ! If there be a ripple now agitating the surface of the stream, trace it up to this fountain-head of *love*.

God is faithful. He cannot deny Himself. He must have some wise end to subserve, if some dark clouds are now intercepting these gracious beams. " For a small moment have I forsaken thee; but with great mercies will I gather thee. In a little wrath I hid my face from thee for a moment ; but with everlasting kindness will I have mercy on thee, saith the Lord thy Redeemer. For this is as the waters of Noah unto me : for as I have sworn that the waters of Noah should no more go over the earth ; so have I sworn that I would not be wroth with thee, nor rebuke thee. For the mountains shall depart, and the hills be removed ; but my kindness shall not depart from thee, neither shall the covenant of my peace be removed, saith the Lord that hath mercy on thee" (Isa. liv. 7-10).

God sets His Bow in the dark sky ; and as if it were not enough that His people should look upon it and take com-

fort in its many and varied promises,—
He Himself graciously becomes a party
in gazing on the covenant pledge ;—
" *And the Bow shall be in the cloud,
AND I SHALL LOOK UPON IT, that I
may remember the everlasting covenant !*" (Gen. ix. 16). He puts Himself
(so to speak) in mind of His own everlasting love. In His Saints' dark and
cloudy day, when they imagine that
their eyes alone are resting on the tokens
of covenant faithfulness, the eye of a
covenant-keeping God is resting upon
them too. ' I will look upon my own
Promises,' He seems to say. ' They
shall be memorials to Myself of My
purposes of unchanging mercy.'

Nor is this love merely a general in-
discriminate affection. The motto-verse
speaks of each individual member of the
Covenant family—" *I have loved* THEE."
" O my Father," says Madame Guyon,
" it seems to me sometimes, as if Thou
didst forget every other being in order

to think only of my faithless and un-grateful heart."

Let us seek to view our trials as so many cords of loving-kindness, by which our God is seeking to draw us, yea, and will draw us nearer Himself. Who knows what mercy may be bound up in what may seem to us dark and mysteri-ous dispensations ? We are apt to mis-name and misinterpret His ways. *We* call His dealings severe trials. *He* calls them " loving-kindnesses."

Drooping saint ! let thine eye rest on the Rainbow over-arching the Throne, spanning from eternity to eternity ; and read for thy comfort the gracious decla-ration—" *The mercy of the Lord is from everlasting to everlasting upon them that fear him.*"

"AND IT SHALL COME TO PASS, WHEN I BRING A CLOUD OVER THE EARTH, THAT THE BOW SHALL BE SEEN IN THE CLOUD."

27TH DAY.

"I do set this Bow in the Cloud"—

" There is a friend that sticketh closer than a brother."
—PROV. xviii. 24.

Inviolable Attachment. CLOSE is that tie which binds brother to brother; the companions of infancy, sharers of one another's joys and sorrows; cast in the same human mould; having engraven on their heart of hearts the same hallowed associations of life's early morning.

But the time for separation at last comes. The birds must leave the parents' nest, and try their pinions beyond their native valley. The world's call to work and warfare is imperious. The old homestead, like a dismembered vessel, is broken to pieces; and the inmates, like that vessel's planks, strew far apart the trough of life's ocean. The world's duties sever some; unhappy estrangements, at times, may sever others; death, at some time, *must* sever all

But there is One whose friendship
and love circumstances cannot estrange,
distance cannot affect, and death cannot
destroy.   The kindest of earthly rela-
tives may say to us regarding this true
Elder Brother, as Boaz said to Ruth,
" It is true that I am thy near kinsman : howbeit there is a Kinsman nearer
than I."   He is Brother, yea, more than
brother ;   Friend, Counsellor, Portion,
Physician,   Shepherd,   all   combined.
Happy for us, when the old avenues of
comfort are closed up, to hear Him,
whose faithfulness is unimpeachable,
saying, " I will not fail thee nor forsake
thee !"   Happy for us when the old
moorings give way, to have One safe
anchorage, that cannot be removed or
shaken.   " I shall now go to sleep,"
said a remarkable saint, who, driven
about with storm and tempest, at last
found the safe Shelter, " I shall now go
to sleep on the Rock of Ages !"

Tried believer, He has never failed

thee, and never will. With Him are no
altered tones, no fitful affections. The
reed may be shaken, but the Rock remains immutable. He is Himself the
true "*Bow in the Cloud.*" The promises of Scripture, like the varied hues
in the natural rainbow, are manifold.
But all these promises are "IN HIM"
(2 Cor. i. 20). Aye, and it is in the
"cloudy day" that this Divine encircling Bow most gloriously appears.
Never should we have known Christ as
"the Brother, born for adversity," unless
by adversity. It is trial that unfolds
and develops His infinite worth and preciousness. When the love of earthly
friends is buried in the grave, the love
of the Heavenly Friend shines forth
more tenderly than ever. As Jonathan
of old, wandering faint and weary in the
wood, found Honey distilling from a
tree and was revived by eating it; so
faint and weary one,—wandering amid
the tangled thickets—the deep glades of

affliction,—seat thyself under thy "Beloved's Shadow with great delight," and let His "fruit be pleasant to thy taste!" This "TREE OF LIFE" distils a balm for every broken, wounded, bleeding heart—every faint and downcast spirit. Yes, JESUS will make, in this the hour of thy loneliness and sorrow, His own life-giving, life-sustaining words and promises, "*sweeter also than honey and the honeycomb.*" Though now exalted on the Throne, "inhabiting the praises of eternity," He still manifests the Brother's heart and the Brother's tenderness. "He is not ashamed to call us brethren."

"AND IT SHALL COME TO PASS,
WHEN I BRING A CLOUD OVER THE EARTH, THAT
THE BOW SHALL BE SEEN IN THE CLOUD."

2 8TH DAY

"I do set this Bow in the Cloud"—

" When thou passest through the waters I will be with
thee; and through the rivers, they shall not overflow
thee: when thou walkest through the fire, thou shalt
not be burned, neither shall the flame kindle upon
thee."—Isa. xliii. 2.

The Supporting
Presence.

WHAT a diversity of
afflictions in this trial-
world !—" Waters, "
" streams," " floods," " flames," " fires."
The Christian is here forewarned that
he will encounter these in some one of
their innumerable phases ; whether it
be loss of health, loss of wealth, loss
of friends, baffled schemes, or blighted
hopes.

But, blessed thought, these trials have
their limits. The *floods* will not " overflow," the *fires* will not " burn," the
flames will not " consume." God will
" stay His rough wind in the day of His
east wind." He will say, " Thus far
shalt thou go, and no farther."

And, better still JESUS will be in all

these trials, and prove sufficient for them all. We shall hear, in the midst " of the great fight of afflictions," the sound of our Master's footsteps. He Himself has passed through these flames, braved these floods, and bared His guiltless head to these storms. He comes to us as He did to His disciples in the very midst of the tempest, and says, "*Fear not,* IT IS I, *be not afraid.*"

Believer, what is your experience ? Is it not that of the triumphant Israelites— "*They went through the flood on foot;* THERE *did we rejoice in Him?*" (Ps. lxvi. 6). " THE FLOOD," the very scene of your trial, you were able to march boldly through it, unappalled by the threatening waves; yea, with your lips vocal with praise ! How this moral heroism—this strange " rejoicing ?" It was because the God of the Pillar-cloud was at your side. Your rejoicing was " in Him." He made you " more than conqueror." You may have many ad-

versaries ranged against you :—" Tribulation, distress, persecution, famine,
nakedness, peril, sword." But there is
ONE in the midst of fires and flames
and floods mightier than all ; and with
Him at your side, you can boldly utter
the challenge to the heights above and
the depths beneath,—" *Who shall separate me from the love of Christ ?* " " Oh,
Sirs," says Thomas Brooks, " there is,
in a crucified Jesus, something propor-
tionable to all the straits, wants, necessities, and trials of His poor people."

"AND IT SHALL COME TO PASS,
WHEN I BRING A CLOUD OVER THE EARTH, THAT
THE BOW SHALL BE SEEN IN THE CLOUD."

29th Day.

"I do set this Bow in the Cloud"—

"We have not an high priest which cannot be touched with the feeling of our infirmities."—Heb. v. 15.

Fellow-Feeling. "As the appearance," says Ezekiel, "of the Bow that is in the cloud in the day of rain, so was the appearance of the brightness round about. This was the appearance of the likeness of the glory of the Lord."

What an elevating truth. *The Sympathy of the God-man-Mediator* (the true Bow in the cloud):—Jesus in our *sorrows!* What a source of exalted joy to the stript and desolate heart!—what a green pasture to lie down upon, amid the windy storm and tempest, or in the dark and cloudy day!

The sympathy of man is cheering and comforting; but "thus far shalt thou go, and no farther." It is finite—limited—often selfish. There are nameless and numberless sorrows on earth, beyond the reach of all human alleviation.

The sympathy of *Jesus* is alone exalted—pure—infinite—removed from all taint of selfishness. He has Himself passed through every experience of woe. There are no depths of sorrow or anguish into which I can be plunged but His everlasting arms are lower still. He has been called "The great sympathetic nerve of His Church, over which the afflictions, and oppressions, and sufferings of His people continually pass." Child of Sorrow, a Human heart beats on the Throne! and He has *thy* name written on that heart. He cares for thee as if none other claimed His regard. As the Great High Priest, He walketh in the midst of his Temple-lamps—(His golden candlesticks,)—plenishing them, at times, with oil;—trimming them, if need be, at others;—but *all* in order that they may burn with a steadier and purer lustre.

" *He was* IN ALL POINTS *tempted.*'
Blessed assurance!—I never can know
the Sorrow into which the " Man of
Sorrows" cannot enter. Ah rather, in
the midst of earth's most lacerating
trials, let me listen to the unanswerable
challenge from the lips of a suffering
Saviour—" *Was there ever any sorrow
like unto* my *sorrow ?*" *He* alone, seemed
to have had the CLOUD without the BOW!
Yet, He refused not to drink the cup of
wrath. He shrunk not back from the
appointed cross. " He set His face
steadfastly to go to Jerusalem ;"—and
even when He hung upon the bitter
tree, He refused the Vinegar that would
have assuaged the rage of thirst and
mitigated physical suffering. Are we
tempted at times to murmur under
God's afflicting hand ? " CONSIDER HIM
that endured, ... *lest ye be weary
and faint in your minds.*" Shall we
hesitate to bear any trial our Lord and
Master sees meet to lay upon us, when

we think of the infinitely weightier Cross
He so meekly and unrepiningly carried
for *us?*

Afflicted one, have thine eye on this
radiant Bow in thy cloud of Sorrow.
Thou mayest, like the disciples on the
Transfiguration-mount, "*fear to enter
the cloud;*"—but hear the voice issuing
from it—"*This is my Beloved Son: hear
Him.*"

Jesus speaks through these clouds.
He tells us *our* cares are *His* cares; *our*
sorrows *His* sorrows. He has some
wise and gracious end in every mysterious chastisement. His language is—
"*Hear ye the rod and who hath appointed it*" (Micah vi. 9). He has too
kind and loving a heart to cause us one
needless or superfluous pang.

Oh that we may indeed *hear* His voice.
Let us not dream that Affliction of itself
is a pathway to Heaven. Clouds do not
form the material Rainbow. These glorious hues come from the Sunbeams alone.

Without the latter, we could discern nothing but blackened heavens and dismal rain-torrents.

It is not because those clad in "white robes" had "come out of *great tribulation*" that they were enjoying the beatific Presence; but because they had "*washed their robes and made them white in the blood of the Lamb*" (Rev. vii. 14). We have only reason to glory in affliction when it has been the means of bringing us nearer the Saviour, and leading us to the opened Fountain.

Jesus! my only hope Thou art,
Strength of my failing flesh and heart;
Oh, could I catch a smile from Thee,
And drop into Eternity!

"AND IT SHALL COME TO PASS,
WHEN I BRING A CLOUD OVER THE EARTH, THAT
THE BOW SHALL BE SEEN IN THE CLOUD."

"I do set this Bow in the Cloud"—

"Yet a little while, and He that shall come will come, and will not tarry."—HEB. x. 37.

A Speedy Coming. "*A* LITTLE *while*," and the unquiet dream of life will be over, and the "morning *without clouds*" shall dawn. A few more tossings on life's tempestuous sea, and the peaceful haven shall be entered. A few more night-watches, and the Lord of love will be seen standing on the Heavenly shore, as once He did on the shores of an earthly lake, with an eternal banquet of love prepared for His "CHILDREN."

Yes, "HE *cometh!*" that is the Church's "blessed hope." It is the voice and presence of her "Beloved" which will "turn the shadow of death into the morning." The dead—the ransomed dead—shall "hear HIS voice and come forth." Those "asleep in Jesus" God is to bring "*with* HIM." His final invit´ tion is not, "Go, ye blessed,

to some bright paradise of angels prepared elsewhere for you ;"—but " Come,
share My bliss—be partakers in *My*
crown :"—" Enter into the joy of your
LORD !" Paul's heaven was described
in two words—" WITH CHRIST." John's
heaven is made up of the two elements
—of likeness *to* Jesus, and fellowship
with Jesus. " We shall be *like* Him,'
" we shall *see* Him as He is." In his
sublime apocalyptic visions, when " the
door was opened in heaven," the first
object which arrests his gaze is, " ONE
who sat upon the throne ;" around whom
was " a *rainbow*, in sight like unto an
emerald " (Rev. iv. 2, 3).

Our happiness will not be complete,
till we are ushered into the full vision
and fruition of Jesus. We are nourished
in this far-off land from " the King's
country ;" but we shall not be satisfied
until we see the King Himself. Jacob
received full waggon loads from Joseph,
but he could not rest till he had seen

him with his own eyes :—when he did
so, the aged man's spirit " revived."
We receive manifold pledges of covenant
mercy from the true Joseph, in this the
house of our pilgrimage ; but we long to
" behold His face in righteousness." We
shall only be " satisfied" when we "awake
in His likeness ! "

" Come ! Lord Jesus, come quickly ! "
He will not tarry.—Each sun, as it sets,
is bringing us nearer the joyful consum-
mation. Time is hastening with gigantic
footsteps, to the advent-throne. The
sackcloth attire of a now burdened
creation, will soon be exchanged for the
full robe of light and beauty which is to
deck a " sabbath-world."

Happy day ! when " the *Bow*," in a
nobler sense, " shall be seen in the
cloud ; "—not the Bow of *Promise*, but
He, in whom all the promises blend
and centre—" *Behold*, HE cometh with
CLOUDS ! "

Seek ever to be in an attitude of

watchfulness. Like the mother of *Sisera*, let faith be straining its ear for the murmur of the chariot-wheels ;—that when the cry shall be heard—" Behold, it is He!" we may be able joyfully to respond—"*Lo! this is our God, we have waited for Him.*"

" Blessed are those servants whom the Lord when He cometh shall find watching : Verily I say unto you, that He shall gird Himself and make them to sit down to meat, and will come forth and serve them."

" AND IT SHALL COME TO PASS,
WHEN I BRING A CLOUD OVER THE EARTH, THAT
THE BOW SHALL BE SEEN IN THE CLOUD."

"I do set this Bow in the Cloud"—

"And the ransomed of the Lord shall return, and come to Zion with songs, and everlasting joy upon their heads: they shall obtain joy and gladness, and sorrow and sighing shall for ever flee away."—ISA. xxxv. 10.

Eternal Joy. BELIEVER, leave thy "*Bow in the cloud*" behind thee; and with thine eye on the "Rainbow round about the throne" (Rev. iv. 3), think of the gladsome return of God's ransomed ones to Zion—every tear-drop dried, every pang forgotten!

Once *wanderers* "in the wilderness, in a solitary way;" prisoners "bound with *affliction* and iron;" *mariners* struggling in a tempest (Ps. cvii. 4, 10, 23); mark the termination of their chequered history. God is not only represented as succouring their fainting souls, shivering in pieces their chains, and enabling them to buffet the angry surges; but He leads the pilgrims to "a city of habitation;" He rescues the captives from " darkness and the shadow of death." He brings the storm-tossed seamen to their " desired haven," and puts the " everlasting song " into the lips of all, " *Oh that men would praise the Lord for his goodness, and for his wonderful works to the children of men !*" (Ps. cvii. 7, 14, 30).

Sorrowing one, tossed on life's stormy sea, soon will that peaceful haven be thine. From the sunlit shores of glory, each and all of thy trials will be seen to be special proofs of thy Heavenly Father's faithfulness,—encircled with a halo of love. Thou mayest now be going forth " weeping," bearing thy precious seed, but thou shalt doubtless come again with *rejoicing*, bringing thy sheaves with thee.

As some seeds require on earth to be steeped in water before they germinate, so is immortal seed ofttimes here steeped in tears. BUT " *they that sow in tears shall reap in* JOY." Though weeping may endure for the night, *joy* cometh in the morning. " You are," says Rutherford, " upon the entry of Heaven's harvest; the losses that I write of are but summer showers, and the Sun of the new Jerusalem shall quickly dry them up." The " song of the night" shall then blend with the song of the skies, and inner, glorious meanings will be disclosed, which are now hidden from the eye of faith.

" *Sorrow and sighing shall for ever flee away!* "

" No sickness, no sorrow, no pain," said an aged saint now entered on these glorious realities ; " but this is only Thy negative. What, O God ! must be Thy positive ? " " *Songs,*" " *everlasting joy,*" " *joy and gladness.*" It will be song upon song, joy upon joy, gladness upon gladness ! These songs of Heaven will be " songs of *degrees.*" The ransomed will be ever graduating in bliss, mounting " from glory to glory," each song

H

suggesting the key-note of a louder and loftier.

Reader, art thou mourning the loss of those who " are not ; " the music of whose voices is hushed for the for-ever of time, and who have left thee to travel companionless and alone the wilderness journey ? A few more fears, a few more tears, and thou shalt meet them in the day-break of glory ! Nay, more ; they have but anticipated thee in an earlier crown. If they have left thee behind, for a little season, to continue thy night-song ; think with bounding heart of that eternal day, when, looking back on the clouds floating in the far distance in the nether Valley, thou shalt be able to join in the anthem, said to be sung by the four-and-twenty elders, as they gaze on the throne encircled by the " RAIN-BOW OF EMERALD ; " for *they* "*rest not day and night, saying,* HOLY, HOLY, HOLY, LORD GOD ALMIGHTY ! " (Rev. iv. 3, 8).

" Lord of our souls !   Thou Saviour ever dear,
    Be still our RAINBOW in the clouds of life ;
  In Thy pure sunlight melt each rising tear,—
    Our Arch of Triumph in the scenes of strife.

" Radiant with mercy, calm the sinking heart,
    And beam through sorrow's night and suffering's
        gloom,
  A deathless Iris that will not depart,
    But shine with hues unfading o'er the tomb !"

" AND

IT SHALL COME TO PASS,

WHEN I BRING A CLOUD OVER THE EARTH,

THAT

THE BOW SHALL BE SEEN IN THE CLOUD :

AND I WILL LOOK UPON IT,

THAT

I MAY REMEMBER

THE EVERLASTING COVENANT,"

PRAYER.

O Lord my God, I desire to draw
near into Thy gracious presence, thank-
ing Thee for Thine infinite and abound-
ing mercies.   Instead of wondering at
Thy chastisements, I have rather reason to marvel at Thy long-suffering
patience, and forbearance, and love.
What are my sorest afflictions compared to what my sins have deserved!
Thou mightst have righteously sent me
the dark cloud, without the Bow of
promise; but Thy ways are not as my
ways, nor Thy thoughts as my thoughts.
I will sing of mercy in the midst of
judgment; unto Thee, O Lord, will I
sing.

I would adore Thy Sovereignty.
"The Lord God omnipotent reigneth."
There is no such thing as accident or
chance with Thee.   It is Thou who
"bringest the cloud over the earth."

It is Thou who alike givest blessings
and takest them away.   Forbid that I
should murmur under Thy righteous
dispensations, or question the rectitude
of Thy dealings.   I may now be unable
to trace the mystery of Thy ways, and
to discern the footsteps of a God of
love.   I may fail to " see the bright
light in the cloud."   Give me grace
to trust Thee : to glorify Thee by im-
plicit faith and unquestioning acquiescence in Thy holy will, saying—
" Even so, Father ; for so it seems
good in Thy sight."

I thank Thee for all Thine exceed-
ing great and precious promises in " the
dark and cloudy day," and especially for
the greatest Gift of Thy love, in the
Adorable Person and meritorious work
of Thine own dear Son.   I have, in
Him, the pledge and guarantee of all
other blessings.   When the tempest
and the earthquake and the whirlwind
are passing by, oh hide me in the clefts

of this Smitten Rock, and enable me to hear " the still small voice." Blessed be Thy name, that while, as God, He is able to *save* to the uttermost,—as Man, He is able to compassionate to the uttermost :—that with infinite tenderness He can enter into all the sorrows and sufferings of His tried and troubled people. Lord, may all Thy dealings serve only to reveal to me more of the preciousness of this Greatest of Sufferers May I feel that His presence and love can compensate for all losses;—that His exalted sympathy can sustain and elevate in the midst of earth's sorest trials; —that His friendship outlasts all that is transient and unstable in a changing world;—that He has turned the very shadow of death into the morning— sanctified the grave, and flooded the Dark valley with hopes full of immortality.

Blessed God, it is behind the cloud Thou oft speakest most tenderly;

teaching precious lessons which in no
way else could be learnt. I know that
when Thy purposes of love are at last
unfolded, I shall see and own all to
have been needed, and all to have been
for the best. Abundantly sanctify present chastisements. May they prove
heart-searchers ; weaning me from
earth, and training me by their salu-
tary discipline for glory. May I hear
in them the needed monitory voice—
" Arise and depart ye, for this is not
your rest." Let me live from day to
day, realising the uncertain and pre-
carious tenure which binds me to
earth's best blessings. Striking, at
Thy command, my pilgrim tent, may I
be enabled to pitch it nearer Heaven
and nearer Thee, — declaring plainly
that I seek " a better country."

Have mercy on the whole family of
the afflicted. When one member suffers, all the members suffer. May the
Holy Spirit, the Comforter, bind up

every bleeding heart. Forbid that they should have the cloud without the bow;—that they should experience Thy chastening hand without the promised consolations;—and instead of exercising unmurmuring submission, harbour suspicions of Thy faithfulness. May they see Thee seated by every furnace, tempering the fury of the flames; may they come forth purified as the gold, and be found more and more meet to stand at last, along with the white-robed multitude who have "come out of great tribulation," in unspotted sanctity before Thy throne.

Lord, let us rejoice in the thought, that the day will speedily arrive, when we shall suffer no more, and sin no more; when trial shall no longer be either felt or feared; when God shall wipe away all tears from off all faces, when the very fountain of weeping shall be for ever dried! Meanwhile, while still in the lower valley,—while

still labourers in the earthly vineyard,—
may we seek to fulfil every needed duty.
Whatever be our appointed work and
warfare, may we be fitted and enabled
to discharge it.   Do Thou mercifully
proportion Thy grace to our season
alike of duty and of trial.   May we
rely on Thine own unchanging promise,
"As thy day is, so shall thy strength
be."   Guide us, good Lord, by Thy
counsel, and afterwards receive us into
Thy glory.

These, and all other needed blessings, I humbly ask, in the name of Him
whom Thou hearest always, —Jesus
Christ, my only Lord and Saviour.
AMEN.

WORDS OF SCRIPTURE.

"THIS IS MY COMFORT IN MY AFFLICTION, FOR THY
WORD HATH QUICKENED ME:"—

"And the Lord said, I have surely seen the affliction of my people, and have heard their cry." "Let us fall now into the hand of the Lord (for His mercies are great), and let me not fall into the hand of man." "He restoreth my soul: He leadeth me in the paths of righteousness, for His name's sake. Yea, though I walk through the valley of the shadow of death, I will fear no evil: for Thou art with me; Thy rod and Thy staff they comfort me." "O my God, my soul is cast down within me: therefore will I remember Thee from the land of Jordan, and of the Hermonites, from the hill Mizar. Deep calleth unto deep at the noise of Thy water-spouts: all Thy waves and Thy billows are gone over me. Yet the Lord will command His loving-kindness in the day-time, and in the night His song shall be with me, and my prayer unto the God of my life. Why art thou cast down, O my soul? and why art thou disquieted within me? hope thou in God: for I shall yet praise Him, who is the health of my countenance, and my God." "How precious also are Thy thoughts unto me, O God! how great is the sum of them!" "He healeth the broken in heart, and bindeth up their wounds." "What shall I say? He hath both spoken unto me, and Himself hath done it: I shall go softly all my years in the bitterness of my soul." "As one whom his mother comforteth, so will I comfort you." "It is of the Lord's mercies that we are not consumed, because His compassions fail not. They are new every morning: great is Thy faithfulness. The Lord is my portion, saith my soul; therefore will I hope in Him. For the Lord will not cast off for ever: but though He cause grief, yet will He have compassion according to the multitude of His mercies." "Therefore, behold, I will allure her, and bring her into the wilderness, and speak comfortably unto her." "The Lord is good, a stronghold in the day of-trouble; and He knoweth them that trust in Him."

"Blessed are they that mourn: for they shall be comforted." "Come unto Me, all ye that labour and are heavy laden, and I will give you rest." "Even so, Father: for so it seemeth good in Thy sight." "But the ship was now in the midst of the sea, tossed with waves: for the wind was contrary. And in the fourth watch of the night Jesus went unto them, walking on the sea. But straightway Jesus spake unto them, saying, Be of good cheer; it is I: be not afraid." "I am the resurrection, and the life: he that believeth in Me, though he were dead, yet shall he live." "Jesus wept." "Said I not unto thee, that, if thou wouldest believe, thou shouldest see the glory of God?" "Let not your heart be troubled: ye believe in God, believe also in Me. In My Father's house are many mansions: if it were not so, I would have told you. I go to prepare a place for you. And if I go and prepare a place for you, I will come again, and receive you unto Myself; that where I am, there ye may be also. And I will pray the Father, and He shall give you another Comforter, that He may abide with you for ever. I will not leave you comfortless: I will come to you. Peace I leave with you, My peace I give unto you: not as the world giveth, give I unto you. Let not your heart be troubled, neither let it be afraid." "Father, I will that they also, whom Thou hast given Me, be with Me where I am; that they may behold My glory." "Who shall separate us from the love of Christ? We are more than conquerors, through Him that loved us."

"But I would not have you to be ignorant, brethren, concerning them which are asleep, that ye sorrow not, even as others which have no hope." "For this corruptible must put on incorruption, and this mortal must put on immortality. So when this corruptible shall have put on incorruption, and this mortal shall have put on immortality, then shall be brought to pass the saying that is written, Death is swallowed up in victory. O death, where is thy sting? O grave, where is thy victory? The sting of death is sin; and the strength of sin is the law. But thanks be to God, which giveth us the victory through our Lord Jesus Christ." "As many as I love, I rebuke and chasten: be zealous therefore, and repent. Behold, I stand at the door, and knock: if any man hear My voice, and open the door, I will come in to him, and will sup with him, and he with Me." "And I heard a voice from heaven saying unto me, Write, Blessed are the dead which die in the Lord from henceforth: Yea, saith the Spirit, that they may rest from their labours; and their works do follow them." "And one of the elders answered, saying unto me, What are these which are arrayed in white robes? and whence came they? And I said unto him, Sir, thou knowest. And he said to me, These are they which came out of great tribulation, and have washed their robes, and made them white in the blood of the Lamb. Therefore are they before the throne of God, and serve Him day and night in His temple: and He that sitteth on the throne shall dwell among them. They shall hunger no more, neither thirst any more; neither shall the sun light on them, nor any heat. For the Lamb which is in the midst of the throne shall feed them, and shall lead them unto living fountains of waters: and God shall wipe away all tears from their eyes."

"WHEREFORE COMFORT ONE ANOTHER
WITH THESE WORDS."

"The sunbeams now are hidden,
    The rains in flood descend;
The winds with angry murmurs,
    The stoutest branches bend.
The radiant face of nature
    Is palled in gloomy shroud;
Yet is the eye directed,
    To look BEYOND THE CLOUD!

"For lo! at length appeareth
    A little streak of light,
Increasing every moment,
    Till all again is bright.
So, dark howe'er our prospects,
    Howe'er by sorrow bowed,
It will not last for ever,—
    We'll look BEYOND THE CLOUD!

"And if the silver lining
    Here faileth to appear;
If stormy skies be o'er us,
    And earth a desert drear:
We'll trust a Father's mercy,
    That ALL has been allowed;
And soon, in His own presence,
    We'll be BEYOND THE CLOUD!"

AND

THERE WAS A

Rainbow

ROUND ABOUT THE THRONE,

IN SIGHT LIKE UNTO

AN

EMERALD.

—*Rev.* iv. 3.

By the same Author.

———◆◆———

Recently published, crown 8vo, 5s. cloth, bevelled edges,

PALMS OF ELIM;

OR, REST AND REFRESHMENT IN THE VALLEYS.

A Companion Volume to the " Grapes of Eshcol."

———————

New Edition, Twelfth Thousand, crown 8vo, 3s. 6d. cloth,

NOONTIDE AT SYCHAR;

OR, THE STORY OF JACOB'S WELL.

A New Testament Chapter in Providence and Grace.

———————

New Edition, Twenty-fourth Thousand, post 8vo,
6s. 6d. cloth,

MEMORIES OF GENNESARET;

OR, OUR LORD'S MINISTRATIONS BY THE SEA OF GALILEE.

With Vignette.

———————

New Edition, Fifth Thousand, crown 8vo, 2s. 6d. cloth,

TALES OF THE WARRIOR JUDGES;

A SUNDAY BOOK FOR BOYS.

———————

Fifth Thousand, crown 8vo, 3s. 6d. cloth extra,

EVENTIDE AT BETHEL;

OR, THE NIGHT-DREAM OF THE DESERT.

An Old Testament Chapter in Providence and Grace.

LaVergne, TN USA
12 October 2009
160628LV00006B/189/A